Electricity

by Carol Levine

PEARSON
Scott
Foresman

DK

What are the effects of moving charges?

Electric Charges

Most atoms have a neutral charge. They have the same number of protons and electrons. Protons have a positive charge, and electrons have a negative charge. The number of protons usually stays the same. But atoms often gain and lose electrons. When this happens, the charge is no longer neutral.

You can see the results of charges moving. If you rub a balloon on clean, dry hair on a dry day, electrons leave your hair. They go to the balloon. The balloon now has more electrons than protons, so it has a negative charge. The balloon will stick to your hair because the hair now has a positive charge. Its charge is positive because it has lost electrons. Opposite charges attract. If you rub two balloons on your hair and then try to put them together, they will push apart. This happens because the balloons have the same charge. Like charges repel.

The flow of charges from your hair to the balloon is electricity. The electricity that flows through wires is called current. **Current** is the flow of electrical charges through a material.

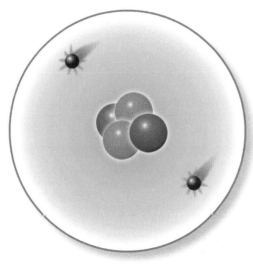

Electrons move around the protons and neutrons of an atom's nucleus.

Conductors

A **conductor** is a material through which electrical charges can flow easily. Conductors have some electrons that are not strongly attached to their atoms. These electrons can move through the conductor.

The more of these free electrons a material has, the better a conductor it is. Metals such as copper, gold, silver, and aluminum are some of the best conductors. Other materials besides metals can be good conductors too. Conductors do not have to be solid either. Some liquids and gases are good conductors.

The salt in ocean water makes it a good conductor. Fresh water is a weak conductor.

A **resistor** is a material that resists, or slows, the flow of electrical charges. Some electrical energy changes into thermal energy as current moves through a resistor. An **insulator** is a material that can stop the flow of current.

Chromium and nickel wires in toasters resist electrical current. They turn the electrical energy into thermal energy. The bread becomes toast because of the heat produced by these resistors.

Usually, most materials have some resistance. Even strong conductors such as gold have a little resistance. Superconductors have no resistance to electrical current. Some metals and ceramics can be superconductors, but only at very, very cold temperatures. Scientists are working to make superconductors that can work at warmer temperatures. The result could be electric devices that use very little energy.

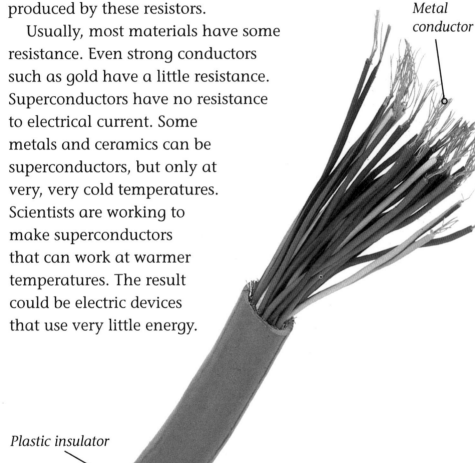

Metal conductor

Plastic insulator

What are simple circuits?

Battery
Batteries provide the energy to move electric charges through this circuit.

Parts of a Circuit

Electric charges move in a circuit. A circuit is a looped path. A simple circuit has an energy source and at least one conductor. It can also have a switch. A switch opens and closes a gap in the conductor. It turns the circuit on or off. Circuits often have resistors too.

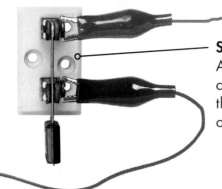

Switch
A switch can turn the circuit on or off.

Insulators
A plastic insulator helps keep the electric charges inside the pathway.

A battery can be the source of energy. The battery has chemicals that react. This reaction produces a current. The current flows from the negative end of the battery to the positive end. Electrical energy is made when the electrical charges flow.

Resistors can change energy into different forms. A light bulb is a resistor. It turns electrical energy into light energy. Some electrical energy changes to heat energy as it flows through a circuit.

Conductor
Conductors, such as metal wires and clips, form a complete loop.

Resistors
This light bulb is a resistor. It changes electrical energy into light energy.

Circuit Diagrams

Circuit diagrams help people build electric circuits. A **circuit diagram** is a map of a circuit. Each part of a circuit is shown by a symbol. The diagram may also have electrical measurements. The electrical energy given by an energy source is measured in **volts.** Many common batteries supply 1.5 volts.

The unit of measure for resistance to electrical current is the ohm. Flashlight bulbs usually have 20 ohms of resistance.

The current in the circuit is measured in amperes, or amps. Current is a measure of how much charge moves past a given spot each second.

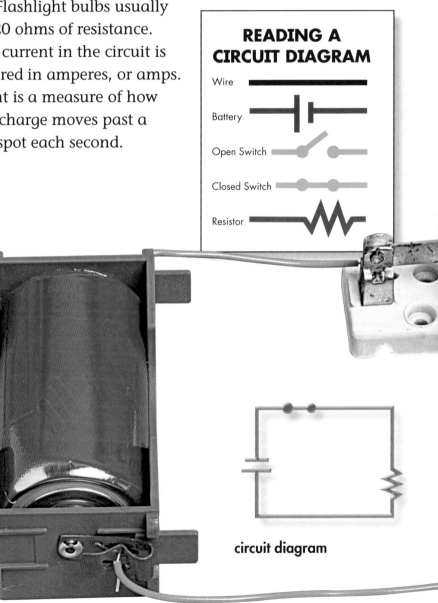

READING A CIRCUIT DIAGRAM

Wire

Battery

Open Switch

Closed Switch

Resistor

circuit diagram

Series Circuits

Series circuits have more than one resistor on a wire. Look at the pictures on this page. They show series circuits with switches, resistors, and batteries in different places.

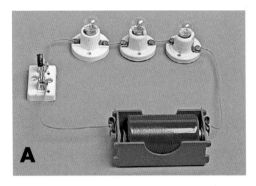

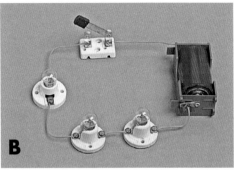

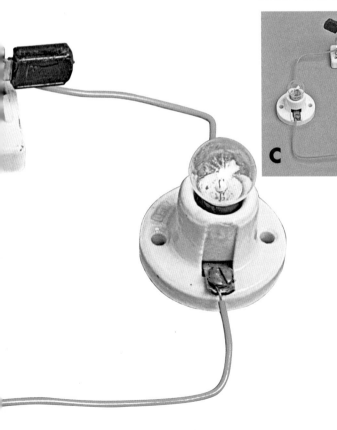

What are complex circuits?

Parallel Circuits

A parallel circuit has more than one branch or pathway. Some circuits have many branches, even hundreds or thousands. Computers have very complicated circuits. Tiny computer chips often have millions of paths and resistors.

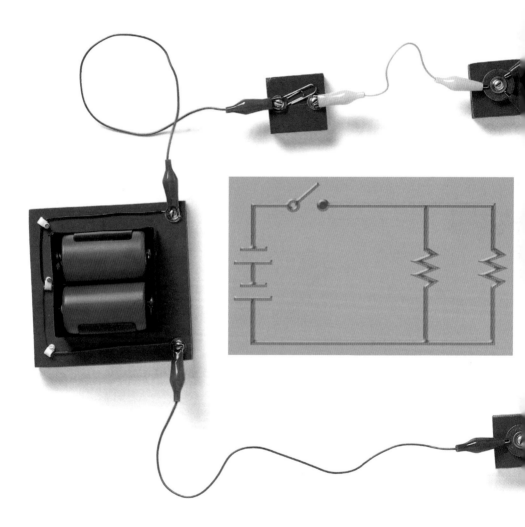

Each branch of a parallel circuit can have several resistors. Electrical energy can be put to work by any of these resistors. Different branches can work at different times. Some can be on while others are off. Switches can control the different paths of a parallel circuit.

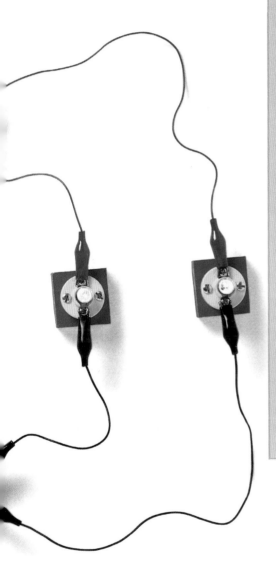

Electrical Safety: Avoid These Shocking Hazards

1. Don't touch electrical outlets. When they are not in use, cover them with safety caps.
2. Always pull the plug instead of the cord. Pulling on the cord can damage the wires.
3. Immediately replace the insulation on a frayed cord.
4. Never touch a power line with your body or any object. Stay far away from downed power lines. If you see one, call 911.
5. Never touch an electrical appliance, switch, cord, plug, or outlet if you or the appliance are standing in water.
6. Do not use cord-operated radios or other electrical appliances near a bathtub, pool, or lake.

Electromagnets

Electricity and magnetism are related. The work of a Danish teacher in 1820 helped us know about the relationship. Every time the teacher flipped the switch on an electric current, he noticed that the needle of a compass moved. The needle was a magnet. He realized that the electric current was producing a magnetic force.

Magnets that carry an electric current are called **electromagnets.** They are made when a current flows through a coiled wire in a circuit.

The electromagnet is strong when there is a large current flowing in the coils.

Electromagnets can be made stronger by increasing the number of coils. They can also be made stronger if a metal bar is placed inside the coils.

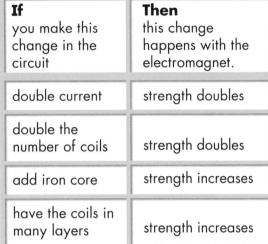

If you make this change in the circuit	Then this change happens with the electromagnet.
double current	strength doubles
double the number of coils	strength doubles
add iron core	strength increases
have the coils in many layers	strength increases

The electromagnet is weaker when the current is less.

Electromagnets are different from regular magnets. An electromagnet can be turned on and off. A regular magnet cannot. The strength of an electromagnet can be changed quickly. The strength of a regular magnet cannot.

But like all magnets, electromagnets have a north pole and a south pole. The magnet is strongest at its poles. It is weaker in between its poles.

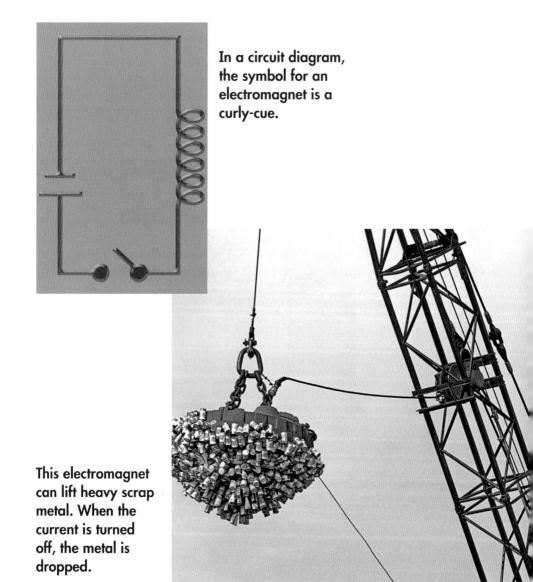

In a circuit diagram, the symbol for an electromagnet is a curly-cue.

This electromagnet can lift heavy scrap metal. When the current is turned off, the metal is dropped.

Ways We Use Electromagnets

We use electromagnets in many everyday objects. In motors, rotating parts spin because electromagnets turn on and off quickly. This causes magnetic fields to attract and repel. Electrical energy is turned into mechanical energy. Motors make many things move, from toys to huge trains. Electromagnets are also used to move parts of doorbells and speakers, producing sound.

The electromagnet pulls the lever arm that hits the bell.

Magnet

Speaker cone

As electromagnets turn on and off quickly, the magnet pushes and pulls on the speaker cone. This causes the cone to vibrate, and these vibrations produce sound waves.

Glossary

circuit diagram   a map of an electric circuit with a symbol for each part

conductor   a material through which an electric charge can move easily

current   the flow of electric charges through a material

electromagnet   a magnet that works because of an electric current

insulator   a material through which heat or electric charge does not flow

resistor   a material or device that resists the flow of an electric charge

volt   a unit measuring the energy available to push an electric charge through a circuit